A QUICK-N-EASY GUIDE TO KEEPING

TROPICAL
FISH

INTERPET PUBLISHING

Different 'windows' present different viewing angles into this spectacular tropical aquarium display – a living picture of an underwater world.

Publishing credits
Editor: Anne McDowall
Consultant: Sean Evans
Photographer: Geoffrey Rogers
Designed and prepress: Stuart Watkinson
Computer graphics: Stuart Watkinson
Production management: Consortium, Poslingford, Suffolk
Print production: Sino Publishing House Ltd, Hong Kong
Printed and bound in China

CONTENTS

Chapter 1: Introducing Tropical Aquarium Fish 4

6 *How fish 'work' – biology and behaviour*
8 *Water – the fish's environment*

Chapter 2: Popular Tropical Aquarium Fish 10

12 *Barbs*
14 *Danios, Minnows and Rasboras*
16 *Tetras*
18 *Catfish*
20 *Anabantids*
22 *Livebearers*

Chapter 3: Setting up a Tropical Aquarium 24

26 *The Tank – choosing and siting*
30 *The Tank – setting up and backgrounds*
32 *Substrates – which type to choose*
34 *Filtration – for good water quality*
36 *Heating and Lighting*
38 *Aquascaping – adding rocks and wood*
40 *Water – treating, adding and testing*
42 *Aquarium Plants – creating a display*
46 *Adding Fish – choosing the right ones*

Chapter 4: Caring for Tropical Aquarium Fish 48

50 *Feeding – for good health*
52 *Routine Aquarium Maintenance*
56 *Health Care – symptoms and cures*

Chapter 5: Developing Your Hobby 60

62 *Breeding Fish – and caring for fry*

64 *Further Information*

Introducing Tropical Aquarium Fish

Understanding where fish come from and how they live

A well-maintained tropical aquarium is a delight to behold and there is now a wide variety of fish from which to choose. It is easy to be tempted by bright colours, fancy fins and unusual appearances, but it is important to remember that these fish come from vastly differing habitats and have different needs in the aquarium. Before you begin to set up an aquarium, it is vital that you have some understanding of how fish live and, most importantly, of their water requirements (see pages 8–9).

Natural habitats

Although all the fish in this book are tropical freshwater species, their distribution and type of habitat vary enormously. Some originate in swift-flowing, cool and highly oxygenated mountain streams, while others make their home in sluggish, poorly oxygenated lower river courses or hot pools that are low in oxygen.

Most aquarium fish are farmed rather than wild caught, but their water requirements remain broadly the same when they are kept in an aqarium. The six species shown opposite are all popular aquarium fish. Although their needs vary somewhat, they could be kept together in slightly hard water with a neutral pH at 23–24°C (73–75°F).

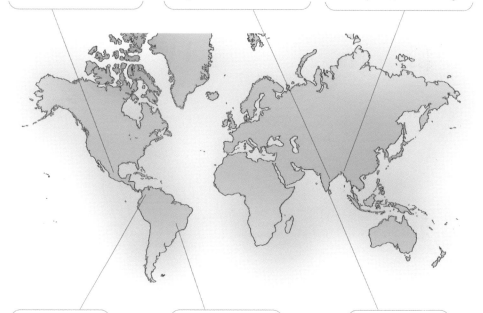

Platy
(see page 22)
Water pH: neutral
Water hardness: slightly hard
Temperature: 21–25°C
(70–77°F)
Origins: Mexico, Guatemala
and Northern Honduras

Zebra Danio
(see page 14)
Water pH: slightly acidic
to neutral
Water hardness: soft to
slightly hard
Temperature: 18–24°C (64–75°F)
Origins: Eastern India

Dwarf Gourami
(see page 20)
Water pH: neutral
Water hardness: soft to
slightly hard
Temperature: 22–28°C (72–82°F)
Origins: India: Ganges,
Brahmaputra, Jumna drainages

Neon Tetra
(see page 16)
Water pH: slightly acidic
to neutral
Water hardness: soft to
slightly hard
Temperature:
20–26°C (68–79°F)
Origins: Peru

Bronze Corydoras
(see page 19)
Water pH: slightly acidic to
slightly alkaline
Water hardness: slightly soft to
slightly hard
Temperature: 22–26°C (72–79°F)
Origins: Trinidad and northern
South America

Cherry Barb
(see page 13)
Water pH: slightly acidic
to neutral
Water hardness: soft to
slightly hard
Temperature: 23–26°C
(73–79°F)
Origins: Sri Lanka

How Fish 'Work' – biology and behaviour

Although the fish you can see displayed in a good aquarium shop may have very different body shapes, all fish have certain things in common and most function in broadly similar ways. It is not essential to have a detailed grasp of fish anatomy, but it does help to know the names of the different fins and other parts of a fish's body that will be referred to elsewhere in the book. It is also helpful to understand why fish behave in certain ways.

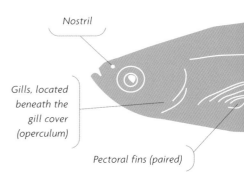

Nostril

Gills, located beneath the gill cover (operculum)

Pectoral fins (paired)

The function of fins

TYPICAL MALE LIVEBEARER

Fish propel themselves through water – which is 800 times denser than air – by means of their flexing body muscles and caudal (or tail) fin. They use other fins for manoeuvring and stability.

Typically fish have seven fins, which are divided into single and paired fins. Single fins include the caudal, dorsal and anal fins, while the pectoral and pelvic, or ventral, fins are paired.

In some fish, some of the fins are modified for other purposes: in male livebearers, for example, the supporting rays of the anal fin are fused to form the gonopodium, which is used for internal fertilization. Other fish, notably catfish, also have fin spines to protect them against predators. The purpose of the adipose fin (see 'Typical armoured catfish', opposite) is unclear.

Gonopodium – fused anal fin used for internal fertilization.

Fish use their tail, or caudal, fin and their powerful, flexible body muscles to propel themselves through the water.

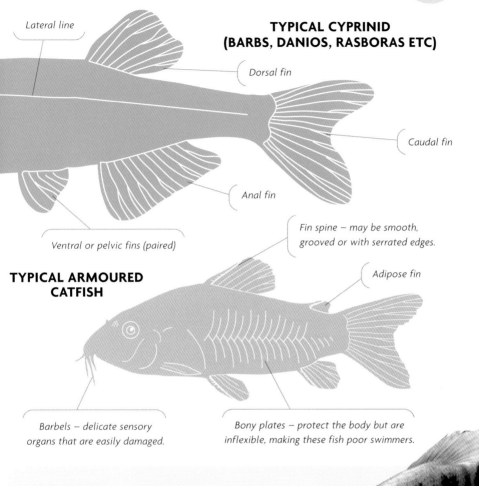

Lateral line

TYPICAL CYPRINID
(BARBS, DANIOS, RASBORAS ETC)

Dorsal fin

Caudal fin

Anal fin

Fin spine – may be smooth, grooved or with serrated edges.

Ventral or pelvic fins (paired)

Adipose fin

TYPICAL ARMOURED
CATFISH

Barbels – delicate sensory organs that are easily damaged.

Bony plates – protect the body but are inflexible, making these fish poor swimmers.

AGGRESSION

As aggression is the most common cause of stress and injuries in an aquarium, it is important to understand the motivation of seemingly bullying fish so that you can deal with it effectively. Some fish will establish feeding or breeding territories and will warn off any intruder. A fish defending its territory will attack only if the intruder does not have sufficient space to distance itself. Make sure your tank is big enough to cope with the territorial nature of some fish.

The other main reason for incompatible behaviour is predation. Clearly, it is foolish to keep a piscivore (fish eater) with other fish that are small enough for it to eat!

*All gouramis are territorial when breeding. This is a Three-spot or Opaline Gourami (*Trichogasater trichopterus*).*

Water – the fish's environment

In any aquarium, the importance of good water quality is paramount – it is the fish's life support. Water needs to be properly filtered to remove harmful ammonia and nitrite from the aquarium, but it also needs to replicate the environmental conditions of the fish in the wild. The most important factors to consider here are pH, hardness and temperature.

The nitrogen cycle

Understanding the nitrogen cycle is the single most important aspect of successful fishkeeping. This is a natural process that occurs in every aquatic habitat around the world. Fish produce ammonia – a poisonous, invisible waste product – which is released into their water. Powered by bacteria, the nitrogen cycle breaks down the ammonia and converts it into less harmful substances, which can then be removed with regular water changes.

Water pH

The pH value is an indicator of the acidity or alkalinity of water. The scale ranges from 0–14, with 0 being extremely acidic and 14 extremely alkaline; 7 represents the neutral point. It is important to understand that the scale is logarithmic, which means that pH 6 is ten times more acidic than pH 7 and 100 times more acidic than pH 8.

In the aquarium, water pH can be affected by biological filtration and the respiration of plants and fish, so it is important to check levels regularly.

THE NITROGEN CYCLE

Nitrates are readily taken up by plants as a food source, usefully reducing the levels in the aquarium.

After digesting nitrogen-rich foods (such as protein), fish excrete extremely toxic ammonia directly from the gills and in urine and faeces. Decomposing biological matter, such as uneaten food and dead leaves, add to the ammonia load.

Nitrobacter and Nitrospira bacteria convert nitrite to nitrate, which is much less harmful to the aquarium fish.

Nitrosomonas bacteria in the biological filter (and coating surfaces in the aquarium) convert ammonia to nitrite, which is still dangerous, even at low concentrations.

This Copper Rosy Barb (Barbus conchonius) prefers slightly acidic water, but, like most barbs, it is quite hardy and will tolerate a relatively wide range of conditions.

pH test kits are available to provide broad-range (shown here) and narrow-range readings. Test pH throughout the life of the aquarium.

Most water hardness test kits are simple colour change kits in which the number of drops required to change the colour of a sample indicates the degree of hardness.

Hard and soft water

Water hardness, measured in degrees (°dH) or sometimes parts-per-million (PPM), is an indicator of the level of dissolved salts in the water: water with a high salt content is referred to as hard; water low in salts as soft.

Water hardness is most commonly divided into General Hardness (GH), which refers mainly to the levels of calcium and magnesium in the water, and Carbonate Hardness (KH), which measures carbonate/bicarbonate and determines how stable the pH is – its 'buffering capacity' or the ability of the water to resist pH changes. Test kits are available for both general and carbonate hardness. The hardness scale ranges from 0°dH (very soft) to 30°dH and above (very hard).

A good test kit will provide advice on suitable fish for a particular hardness and on how to change the hardness if required.

Popular Tropical Aquarium Fish

Choosing the best first fish for a new aquarium

Visit a good aquarium shop and you will see a huge variety of tropical fish of all shapes, sizes and colours for sale. But, particularly if you are new to fishkeeping, how do you decide which ones to choose? This chapter provides a guide to some of the most popular fish groups and species that are ideal for the community aquarium. Most of the fish illustrated here are very peaceable and are suitable for the beginner, though not all should be added early on. Before you make your selection, you will need to establish your aquarium and check the maximum stocking levels for the size of your tank. You will also need to make sure that you introduce the fish gradually. (See pages 29, 46 and 49 for further information.)

Compatibility

Choosing fish for a community aquarium involves taking into account the needs of a particular species as well as considering their compatibility with other fish. Many of the smaller fish illustrated in this chapter – notably barbs, tetras, danios and rasboras – are shoaling fish that should be kept in groups of at least four to six; others, such as Corydoras catfish and the Dwarf Gourami, are happiest in a pair or trio; while a male Siamese Fighting Fish is best kept on its own.

Sizes of fish

It is important that you don't exceed the recommended stocking levels for the size of your tank (see page 29). When calculating the number of fish you can accommodate, don't forget to allow for their growth if the fish you are buying are not fully mature.

You will also need to consider the relative size of your chosen fish: a large peaceful fish may still be too boisterous for much smaller species. Remember, as well, that a fish may be only as safe as the size of its mouth!

These fast-moving Neon Tetras need to be kept in a group of at least four to six. A group of a dozen or more will provide a truly spectacular display.

tip

Check before you choose

Don't be seduced by beautiful colours and strange appearances – check the specific requirements and temperament of a species with your aquarium dealer before you buy it to make sure that it is suitable for your aquarium and its existing occupants.

LEVELS IN THE AQUARIUM

The top 5cm (2in) of water is home to species that swim and feed at the surface, such as gouramis (see pages 20–1).

The middle layer is the largest zone in the tank. This is where you will find shoaling fish such as barbs (see pages 12–13) and tetras (see pages 16–17).

The bottom layer of the tank is inhabited by foragers such as catfish (see pages 18–19) and loach (see page 15).

Barbs

These very popular aquarium fish, members of the carp (Cyprinidae) family, have the classic streamlined fish shape of shoaling midwater fishes. Most barbs are good fish for beginners to fishkeeping: they feed on small aquatic insects, crustaceans and some plant matter and most have no special maintenance requirements.

Arulius Barb

Barbus arulius
Mature size: 12cm (4³/₄in)
One of the largest barb species, the Arulius Barb is best kept in a large community aquarium, which should include a few others of the same species. As the largest of the barbs featured here, it is best kept with other medium to large robust species. Mature fish develop a distinctive blue-purple pattern along the back.

OTHER POPULAR BARBS

- Blue-barbed Barb *(Barbus barilioides)*
- Cuming's Barb *(Barbus cumingi)*
- Clown Barb *(Barbus everetti)*
- Black-spot Barb *(Barbus filamentosus)*
- Striped Barb *(Barbus lineatus)*
- Black Ruby Barb *(Barbus nigrofasciatus)*
- Checkered Barb *(Barbus oligolepis)*
- Pentazona Barb *(Barbus pentazona pentazona)*
- Golden Barb *(Barbus semifasciolatus)*
- Odessa Barb *(Barbus ticto)*

Tiger Barb

Barbus tetrazona
Mature size: 7cm (2³/₄in)
Although the Tiger Barb is a very popular aquarium fish thanks to its distinctive striped pattern, it does have a reputation for fin-nipping. This aggressive behaviour seems to be less of a problem if it is kept in a shoal of at least six.

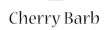

Cherry Barb

Barbus titteya
Mature size: 5cm (2in)
The small Cherry Barb from Sri Lanka is happiest when kept in a small shoal – though it will survive happily in a pair – in an aquarium with plenty of plant cover. At spawning time, males develop a deep red coloration, which gives the species its common name.

tip *Provide cover*
Most barbs appreciate hiding places in the aquarium so make sure there is sufficient plant cover as well as plenty of swimming space for these fast movers.

Rosy Barb

Barbus conchonius
Mature size: 7cm (2³⁄₄in)
This lively and boisterous fish might be a bit much for more placid species, but, with its bright colours, it is nevertheless a popular choice for a smaller aquarium. Like most other barbs, it is best kept in a shoal and needs a certain amount of plant cover and enough swimming space.

Danios, Minnows and Rasboras

These small, fast-swimming shoaling fish will occupy the often under-populated middle layers of the aquarium. Like barbs, they are generally peaceable and make ideal subjects for a community aquarium. They are also inexpensive and hardy and so perfect first fish for the new fishkeeper.

This group includes some of the easiest aquarium fish to breed – the Zebra Danio and the White Cloud Mountain Minnnow.

Harlequin Rasbora

Trigonostigma heteromorpha
Mature size: 4.5cm (1³⁄₄in)
The most commonly kept rasbora, the Harlequin is an attractive and peaceful fish best kept in a large shoal. The characteristic black triangle on the rear half of the body has a straight front edge on females, which are also deeper bodied than males.

Zebra Danio

Danio rerio
Mature size: 6cm (2¹⁄₂in)
Among the most popular and least expensive of all aquarium fish, the Zebra Danio is extensively farmed and long-finned variants are common. It is also one of the easiest aquarium fish to breed. The Leopard Danio is similar but has spots along its flanks instead of stripes.

Giant Danio

Devario aequipinnatus
Mature size: 10cm (4in)
Because of its size, the Giant Danio needs a larger, planted aquarium. In its natural habitat it lives in fast-running water and so needs good aeration in the aquarium. It swims near the surface and is also a keen jumper, so make sure that the tank is tightly covered.

White Cloud Mountain Minnow

Tanichthys albonubes
Mature size: 4cm (1½in)
Another attractive, peaceful fish, the White Cloud Mountain Minnow has white stripes along its flanks and striking red and white fins. Although a long-finned variety has been developed, the original form is still favoured. As with danios and rasboras, this fish needs to be kept in a shoal: a lone individual may become timid and lose its colour.

Pearl Danio

Danio albolineatus
Mature size: 6cm (2½in)
Like the Zebra Danio, the Pearl Danio has a pearly iridescence shot through with blue and purple. Females are larger and more colourful than males. Colour varieties are available, including the golden one shown here. Like other danios, it is best kept in a shoal, is a fast swimmer and likes to jump.

LOACHES

Belonging to a family related to barbs and danios, loaches are generally peaceful and some species make ideal additions to a community aquarium. Among the most popular are the Clown Loach (*Chromobotia macracanthus*), shown below, the Dwarf or Chain Loach (*Yasuhikotakia sidthimunki*) and the Coolie Loach (*Pangio kuhlii*).

Loaches have evolved as bottom-feeders – in the aquarium they forage on the substrate, where they feed on particles of food missed by other fish.

15

Tetras

Like barbs, tetras are small, peaceable, shoaling fish that are perfect for the community aquarium, where their bright, jewel-like colours seem to light up the display. Thanks to intensive farming, these beautiful fish are also inexpensive and are highly adaptable to aquarium conditions. Most species like a heavily planted aquarium, which will mimic their natural, mostly Amazonian, habitat of woodland streams.

OTHER POPULAR TETRAS

- Black Widow Tetra (*Gymnocorymbus ternetzi*)
- Silver-tipped Tetra (*Hasemania nana*)
- Buenos Aires Tetra (*Hemigrammus caudovittatus*)
- Head-and-Tail Light Tetra (*Hemigrammus ocellifer*)
- Serpae Tetra (*Hyphessobrycon callistus*)
- Flame Tetra (*Hyphessobrycon flammeus*)
- Black Neon Tetra (*Hyphessobrycon herbertaxelrodi*)
- Red-eyed Tetra (*Moenkhausia sanctaefilomenae*)
- Emperor Tetra (*Nematobrycon palmeri*)
- Congo Tetra (*Phenacogrammus interruptus*)

Neon Tetra

Paracheirodon innesi
Mature size: 5cm (2in)
Like several other tetras, the Neon appears to be lit from within and its iridescent coloration appears to best effect in a large shoal seen darting through dense plant cover. Avoid housing them with larger fish, particularly Angelfish, which may eat them.

Glowlight Tetra

Hemigrammus erythrozonus
Mature size: 4cm (1½in)
The red stripes down the flanks of this striking fish appear to glow from within and may assist shoals in the wild to stay close together. In the aquarium, keep these fish in groups of at least six. Their colours look brightest against dense planting, which these fish prefer.

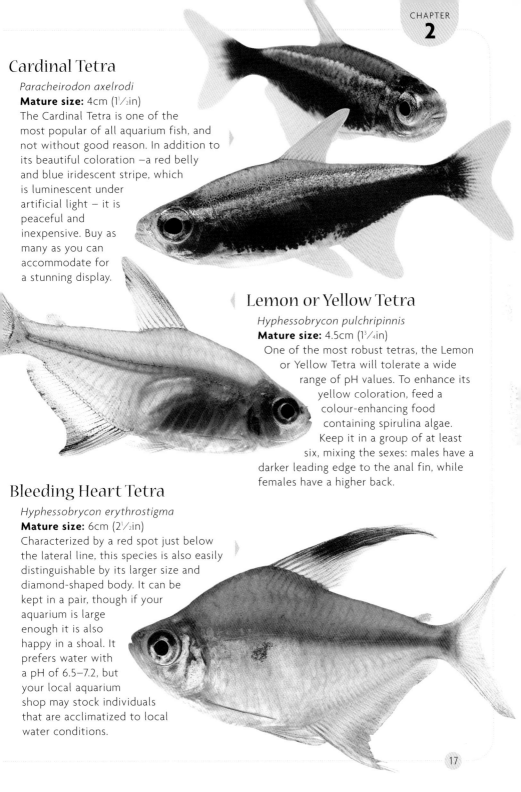

Cardinal Tetra

Paracheirodon axelrodi
Mature size: 4cm (1½in)
The Cardinal Tetra is one of the
most popular of all aquarium fish, and
not without good reason. In addition to
its beautiful coloration – a red belly
and blue iridescent stripe, which
is luminescent under
artificial light – it is
peaceful and
inexpensive. Buy as
many as you can
accommodate for
a stunning display.

Lemon or Yellow Tetra

Hyphessobrycon pulchripinnis
Mature size: 4.5cm (1¾in)
One of the most robust tetras, the Lemon
or Yellow Tetra will tolerate a wide
range of pH values. To enhance its
yellow coloration, feed a
colour-enhancing food
containing spirulina algae.
Keep it in a group of at least
six, mixing the sexes: males have a
darker leading edge to the anal fin, while
females have a higher back.

Bleeding Heart Tetra

Hyphessobrycon erythrostigma
Mature size: 6cm (2½in)
Characterized by a red spot just below
the lateral line, this species is also easily
distinguishable by its larger size and
diamond-shaped body. It can be
kept in a pair, though if your
aquarium is large
enough it is also
happy in a shoal. It
prefers water with
a pH of 6.5–7.2, but
your local aquarium
shop may stock individuals
that are acclimatized to local
water conditions.

Catfish

Catfish are incredibly diverse: the 34 catfish families have colonized all tropical and temperate regions and species range in size from less than 5cm (2in) to more than 1.5m (5ft). What they all have in common is a lack of scales – they are either naked or covered with bony plates – and 'whiskers', known as 'barbels', which give these fish their name.

Corydoras are the most popular of all aquarium catfish and are unfairly known as the 'hoovers' of the catfish world because they forage on the substrate for leftovers. To maintain their barbels in good condition, Corydoras catfish should be kept in an aquarium with a sandy substrate.

Sterba's Corydoras

Corydoras sterbai
Mature size: 6cm (2½n)
This beautiful Corydoras catfish, with its distinctively and evenly spotted pattern, is a community favourite. To help it feel at home in the aquarium, provide it with an area of open substrate to swim around.

Bristlenose Catfish

Ancistrus temminckii
Mature size: 12cm (4¾in)
This superb example of a suckermouth catfish is distinguished by the bristles on its nose, which help this bottom-dwelling fish find its way around when visibility is poor. Provide it with plenty of hiding places in the aquarium.

OTHER POPULAR CATFISHES

- *Corydoras duplicareus*
- *Corydoras gossei*
- Harald Schultz's Corydoras (*Corydoras haraldschultzi*)
- Peppered Corydoras (*Corydoras paleatus*)
- Dwarf Corydoras (*Corydoras pygmaeus*)
- *Corydoras reticulatus*
- Twig Catfish (*Farlowella vittata*)
- Zebra or Imperial Plec (*Hypancistrus zebra*) (see page 61)
- Glass Catfish (*Kryptopterus bicirrhis*)
- Dwarf Otocinclus (*Otocinclus affinis*)
- Clown Plec (*Peckoltia vittata*)

Panda Corydoras

Corydoras panda
Mature size: 5cm (2in)
It is easy to see where this small catfish gets its name: the black mask, which runs from the top of its head down through the eyes, lends it a very panda-like appearance.
Corydoras catfish never thrive as individuals: buy a pair or small group if you can.

Bronze Corydoras

Corydoras aeneus
Mature size: 7cm (2¾in)
This is perhaps the most common of all aquarium catfish and a popular choice for beginners. This armoured catfish likes to forage in open areas of substrate and will keep foreground plants free of debris. An attractive albino form is also available (see left).

Anabantids

These fish are more commonly known as labyrinth fish, the 'labyrinth' being a respiratory organ located above each gill chamber, which enables these fish to breathe atmospheric oxygen. This ability has meant that anabantids can survive in roadside ditches and rice paddies, where pollution and a lack of oxygen in the water would spell disaster for most other fish species. Most aquarium anabantids are small, brightly coloured and relatively easy to keep and breed, though all benefit from mature water, so wait a while before introducing them to your aquarium.

Siamese Fighting Fish

Betta splendens
Mature size: 7cm (2³⁄₄in)
The Siamese Fighting Fish is undeniably beautiful, but it is short-lived – two years is a good age. A sole male – only males have these spectacular flowing fins – will survive peacefully in a community aquarium (as long as there are no potential fin-nippers), but never keep males together or ferocious attacks will soon develop. A breeding pair will need a well-planted tank to themselves.

Dwarf Gourami

Colisa lalia
Mature size: 5cm (2in)
A humped shoulder profile is typical of these peaceable, if somewhat shy, fish. Numerous aquarium variants include cobalt blue (shown here) and royal red forms. Dwarf Gouramis survive best when kept as a pair: males (shown here) are more colourful than the females.

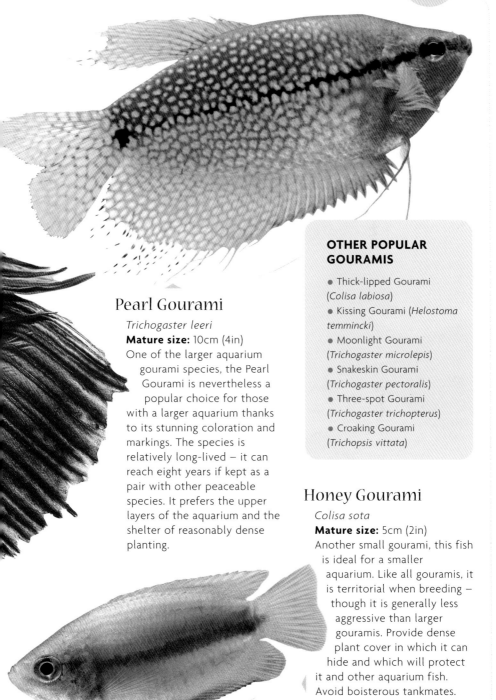

Pearl Gourami

Trichogaster leeri
Mature size: 10cm (4in)
One of the larger aquarium gourami species, the Pearl Gourami is nevertheless a popular choice for those with a larger aquarium thanks to its stunning coloration and markings. The species is relatively long-lived – it can reach eight years if kept as a pair with other peaceable species. It prefers the upper layers of the aquarium and the shelter of reasonably dense planting.

OTHER POPULAR GOURAMIS

- Thick-lipped Gourami (*Colisa labiosa*)
- Kissing Gourami (*Helostoma temmincki*)
- Moonlight Gourami (*Trichogaster microlepis*)
- Snakeskin Gourami (*Trichogaster pectoralis*)
- Three-spot Gourami (*Trichogaster trichopterus*)
- Croaking Gourami (*Trichopsis vittata*)

Honey Gourami

Colisa sota
Mature size: 5cm (2in)
Another small gourami, this fish is ideal for a smaller aquarium. Like all gouramis, it is territorial when breeding – though it is generally less aggressive than larger gouramis. Provide dense plant cover in which it can hide and which will protect it and other aquarium fish. Avoid boisterous tankmates.

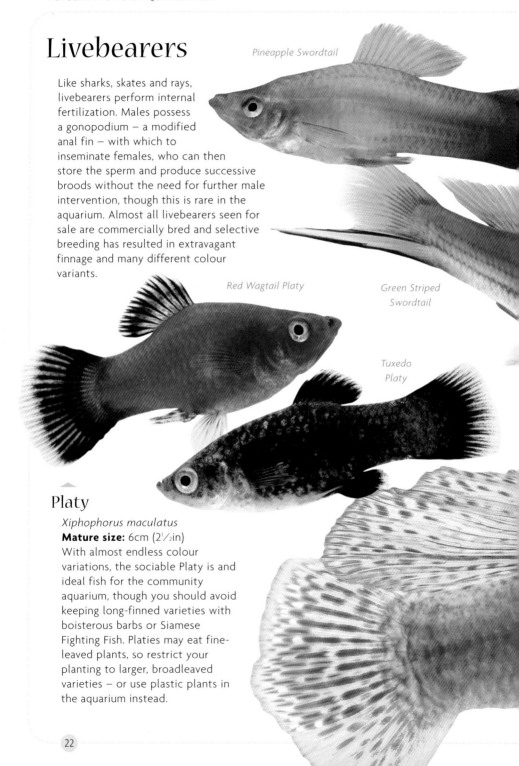

Livebearers

Pineapple Swordtail

Like sharks, skates and rays, livebearers perform internal fertilization. Males possess a gonopodium – a modified anal fin – with which to inseminate females, who can then store the sperm and produce successive broods without the need for further male intervention, though this is rare in the aquarium. Almost all livebearers seen for sale are commercially bred and selective breeding has resulted in extravagant finnage and many different colour variants.

Red Wagtail Platy

Green Striped Swordtail

Tuxedo Platy

Platy

Xiphophorus maculatus
Mature size: 6cm (2½in)
With almost endless colour variations, the sociable Platy is and ideal fish for the community aquarium, though you should avoid keeping long-finned varieties with boisterous barbs or Siamese Fighting Fish. Platies may eat fine-leaved plants, so restrict your planting to larger, broadleaved varieties – or use plastic plants in the aquarium instead.

Swordtail

Xiphophorus helleri
Mature size: males: 10cm (4in)
The Swordtail inhabits the middle and upper levels of the aquarium and is generally peaceful, though provide plenty of cover if you have more than one male as they can become antagonistic towards each other. The wild fish is an unexceptional green, but breeders have produced many striking colour varieties. Mature males have the long, swordlike extension of the lower lobe of the tail fin; females, which are just as brightly coloured, are larger and more thickset.

Guppy

Poecilia reticulata
Mature size: 6cm (2½in)
Originally from Central America, guppies will be happy in a wide temperature band (18−28°C/64−82°F), given hard, neutral to alkaline water. These peaceful fish occupy the middle and upper layers of the tank and are ideal for the community aquarium, but avoid keeping them with boisterous barbs or with male Siamese Fighting Fish of the same coloration, which may mistake them for rivals and attack them.

King Cobra Guppy

Neon Blue Guppy

Sailfin Molly

Poecilia velifera
Mature size: 18cm (7in)
The natural coloration is a mix of green, yellow and silver but colour varieties are also available. The male of the species has a spectacularly long dorsal fin (hence its common name), which extends the mottled pattern of the body and is edged with gold. This is a peaceful fish but avoid keeping it with potential fin-nippers.

Orange Sailfin Molly

Setting Up a
Tropical Aquarium

Creating a safe and healthy home for your fish

Before you buy your fish, you will need to prepare carefully for their arrival. Establishing an aquarium takes time – and some financial outlay – and this process should not be hurried. The aquarium water will need time to stabilize after you have set up the tank before you can introduce your first fish – we have already seen the importance of good water quality for fish. You will also need to work out how big a tank you can afford – don't forget to budget for heating, lighting, a filtration system and tank décor too (see opposite) – and find the best location for it.

EQUIPMENT CHECKLIST

Once established, tropical aquarium fish are relatively inexpensive to maintain but before you begin you will need to plan for the necessary aquarium equipment and furnishings. Don't skimp on the following:

Background (see page 31)
Some are solid panels that need to be added at the start; others stick to the back of the tank.

Tank (see page 28)
Make sure that it is large enough and that you have an appropriate place to site it.

Décor (see pages 38–39)
A naturalistic display like this one should include some large and small rocks and bits of driftwood, but more fun items are also available.

Lighting (see page 37)
Many modern aquariums have lighting concealed within an integral hood.

Heater-thermostat (see page 36)
A combined heater-thermostat is the ideal choice if you are new to fishkeeping, but you may want to investigate other options.

Stand or cabinet (see page 29)
A full tank is very heavy. Unlike most domestic furniture, a purpose-built stand will be able to withstand its weight.

Filtration system (see pages 34–35)
Various types are available, including internal and external ones.

Substrate (see pages 32–33)
Options include different grades – as well as colours – of gravel, sand and polished pebbles.

Plants (see pages 42–45)
Do you want to have real plants in the aquarium or use plastic ones?

The Tank – choosing and siting

It's easy to think about how many fish you would like to keep and decide on a big tank on that basis. In fact, your first consideration will need to be where you can place the aquarium in your home. How much space you have – in a suitable location – will dictate the size and shape of aquarium you can accommodate.

Choosing a location

Its location will have a great influence on how successful your aquarium is. You will, of course, need to think about practical considerations: make sure there are adequate electrical sockets nearby and avoid sites where the fish will be disturbed by noise or where direct sunlight, draughts or heat from radiators will cause fluctuations in the water temperature. But you will also want to choose a focal point for the aquarium in a room where people spend the most time relaxing in the evenings or at mealtimes. You may want to think about using a large aquarium as a room divider, where it can be viewed from both sides, or to set it into a wall to provide the classic 'living picture'.

A rectangular aquarium provides a spectacular display. If you have the space, why not locate it so that it can be viewed from several sides, perhaps as a room divider.

SITING THE AQUARIUM

Dimmer switches fitted to lights will help reduce shock to the fish of a sudden change between darkness and bright light.

Avoid siting the tank in direct sunlight. Not only will this raise the water temperature, but it will also stimulate unsightly algae growth.

Draughty areas, such as near windows or doors, will also cause fluctuating water temperatures. In addition, doors opening and closing suddenly can stress fish.

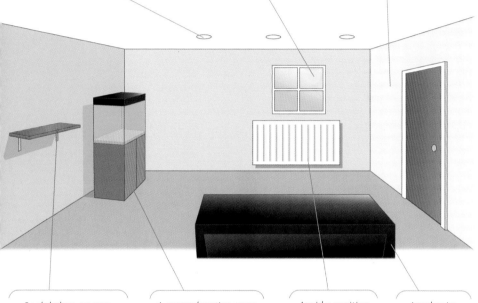

Bookshelves, or even larger pieces of furniture, are generally unsuitable for an aquarium, which is very heavy once filled. Purpose-built shelves may be used if the loading is carefully calculated beforehand.

A corner location away from draughts is ideal for the aquarium. Make sure you have electrical sockets nearby, but not directly beneath.

Avoid a position close to a radiator or fireplace as this will affect the water temperature.

Loud noise levels from a TV or loudspeakers will also stress your fish.

tip *Check access*

Make sure not only that you have found a suitable place for the aquarium but also that you can get it into the room through doorways.

Providing support

A filled tank is extremely heavy (see page 29) and your floor, as well the furniture on which you place the tank, must be able to support this weight. If you have a concrete floor, this should pose no problems, but if you have floorboards, try to position the stand so that the weight of the finished unit is taken by the joists and not the floorboards.

Choosing a tank

Although you will want your aquarium to look aesthetically pleasing, your first thought should be for your fish: your chosen style must provide the correct conditions for them to survive. A good design will have a large surface area to allow sufficient exchange of gases. (Like humans, fish 'breathe' oxygen and 'exhale' carbon dioxide and these gases are dissolved in the water and get in and out at the surface.)

*These Pentazona Barbs (*Barbus pentazona pentazona*) are fast-moving shoaling fish that need plenty of swimming space. Don't forget to allow for the fact that young fish will grow.*

SUITABLE TANK STYLES

Cube aquariums provide great opportunities for creative planting and interesting viewing aspects, along with an acceptable surface area in relation to depth.

The most effective and compelling format – and a traditional choice – is the rectangular aquarium, which provides a 'widescreen' landscape view and a large surface area in relation to the volume of water. Rectangular aquariums are available in a range of sizes.

A variation on the standard rectangular tank, this bow-fronted aquarium is supplied with a purpose-built stand and with lighting and filtration included. Corner-shape units are also available, as are six-sided aquariums.

SIZE AND CAPACITIES OF STANDARD TANKS

Tank	Volume	Weight of water	Fish length*
60x30x30cm (24x12x12in)	55 litres (12 gallons)	55kg (120lb)	55cm (22in)
60x30x38cm (24x12x15in)	68 litres (15 gallons)	68kg (150lb)	68cm (27in)
90x30x30cm (36x12x12in)	82 litres (18 gallons)	82kg (180lb)	82cm (32in)
90x30x38cm (36x12x15in)	104 litres (23 gallons)	104kg (230lb)	104cm (41in)
120x30x30cm (48x12x12in)	109 litres (24 gallons)	109kg (240lb)	109cm (43in)
120x30x38cm (48x12x15in)	136 litres (30 gallons)	136kg (300lb)	136cm (54in)

*Total length excluding tail

Stands and cabinets

Your chosen style of tank may come with its own stand – or you may be able to buy one separately to match it. In any case, you will need to consider how you are going to support the tank – domestic furniture is unlikely to be able to bear the weight (see the table above).

Flat-packed or ready-made cabinets are usually available in a choice of styles and finishes. Some have cupboards below in which you can conceal lighting units, external filters and cables.

Buy big!

Choose the biggest tank that you can afford and have space to accommodate. The larger the volume of water, the easier it will be to control the waste products the fish produce and hence provide a stable environment.

Integrated tanks and cabinets like this are designed as pieces of furniture and come in a choice of veneers. Cut-outs at the back allow for cables, filter pipes, etc.

The hood of the cabinet contains sliding glass trays that form a condensation tray and give access to the tank. There is space at the rear of the hood for the lighting unit.

The Tank – setting up and backgrounds

Whatever size aquarium you have chosen, it and its stand will be awkward and heavy and you will need someone to help you to set them up. Make sure that the room you are working in is clear of clutter and other people and pets. Remove any rugs or loose floor coverings.

Unpack the stand and tank and rest the tank on some polystyrene tiles on the floor to avoid damaging the base. (It may crack if the floor is uneven.) Assemble the stand or cabinet (if flat-packed) following the manufacturer's instructions and place it into position.

SETTING UP THE STAND

Stands are usually either metal box sections supplied flat-packed or one-piece pressed-steel types. Flat-pack types slot together but may need a little gentle encouragement with a mallet. (Place a piece of board between the mallet and the stand to avoid damaging it.) If you use a metal stand rather than a wood cabinet, it is usually necessary to place a piece of board on top, with a layer of polystyrene between the tank base and the board.

Levelling the tank and stand

Using a spirit level, make sure that the stand is level from side to side and back to front. A tank that is not level will not only look unsightly but will also be potentially unstable. Some stands have feet that you can adjust by screwing them up or down.

If you are planning to use the type of flexible plastic background that attaches to the rear of the aquarium, you will need to fix it in place before you position the tank. Cut the background to size before fixing it.

Place a sturdy baseboard of melamine-coated chipboard on top of the stand and add a single layer of polystyrene tiles, accurately trimmed to the size of the tank base. If you wish you can disguise the white edges with black insulation tape. Position the tank on top and clean it with a new cloth and water – avoid using any detergent.

BACKGROUNDS

Adding a background to an aquarium can help to enhance the finished display and disguise the wall behind it. The best ones are plastic and available on a roll, so they are waterproof and easy to cut to size. You can choose a solid colour – black will bring out the colours of plants and fish and is available with blue on the reverse side – or a picture background, such as the trees and logs, sunken city, rockwork or plant scenes shown below.

Attach the background to the back of the tank on the outside using double-sided adhesive tape along the entire length of each side or sticky pads at each corner.

For the most effective display, co-ordinate your background with the style of your other tank decorations.

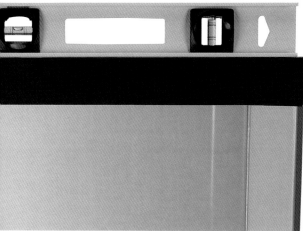

Once the tank is in position, check that it is completely level – back to front and side to side – using a long spirit level.

Adjust the stand not the tank

Placing wedges under a glass tank full of water will create stresses that may cause the glass to fracture.

Substrates – which type to choose

Your aquarium dealer should stock a variety of materials suitable for use on the aquarium floor, the most commonly available of which is pea gravel. These rounded, pealike grains are available in a range of particle sizes, the most useful of which is 5mm (1/4in). This grade has an open structure and will not pack down too tightly, allowing oxygenated water to slowly circulate to all levels. Pea gravel may be unsuitable if you need to provide slightly acidic conditions, however, because of its mineral content.

Adding substrate to the tank

All substrate materials will need to be washed before use. Place the substrate, a small amount at a time, into a bucket of water and agitate it to remove any dirt. Repeat until the water runs clear.

Add the substrate to the aquarium with your hands or using a jug to a depth of about 4–5cm (1 1/2–2in). Slope it towards the back of the tank if you wish.

SUITABLE SUBSTRATE MATERIALS

Lime-free gravel
A good planting medium and completely inert so will not affect your water chemistry in any way.

Pea gravel
Commonly available and cheap to buy. Mixed grades add variety and combine well with larger pebbles and rocks.

Red chippings
Add colour and texture and are available in other colours – choose ones that match the rocks in your tank.

Black quartz
Makes a good contrast to the more usual golden brown colour.

Lava rock
Made by firing clay material at very high temperatures to produce inert rocklike fragments with a large surface area.

River sand soon compacts down, but it is the best substrate for catfish. If you choose a sandy substrate, disturb it regularly with your fingers to prevent stagnation. Clear away algae and debris with a clear siphon tube.

ADDING NUTRIENTS TO THE SUBSTRATE

Unfortunately, most aquarium substrates, including gravel, do not contain any nutrients and cannot sustain plants on their own, so you will need to add a food source to ensure healthy plant growth. There are many long-term plant food supplements on the market that are added directly to the substrate. Some of these need to be used in conjunction with a bacterial culture that will release the nutrients in a form that plants can use.

Sprinkle the supplement evenly over the surface of the gravel. If a bacterial culture is also supplied, crumble this between your fingers and add a thin layer on top. Gently mix the ingredients into the substrate with your fingers, smooth over the top and add a final layer of substrate to the required depth. This will sustain the plants for several months, after which time you will need to add fertilizer tablets close to the plant roots to continue feeding them.

Filtration – for good water quality

There are two basic types of filtration systems available: internal and external. Both are designed to perform the same basic functions. Firstly, the filter removes solid waste from the water; secondly, it provides a large surface area bathed with oxygenated water that will stimulate the growth of millions of beneficial 'cleaning' bacteria (see page 8); thirdly, it removes specific wastes or toxic products from the water with chemical filter media.

Internal power filters

Unless you have a large aquarium (i.e. over 180 litres/40 gallons), a compact internal power filter that will sit discreetly in the back corner of your aquarium will normally be adequate. (Bear in mind,

however, that it is always better to use a filter that is slightly larger and more powerful than the minimum size recommended for your tank.)

In this type of system, a submersible water pump at the top of the unit draws water through the filter medium and circulates it back into the tank. Regular maintenance of the unit is vital to ensure that the solid waste trapped in the filter foam does not build up to a level that impedes the growth of filtration bacteria (see page 53).

tip *Never run the pump out of water*

If you want to test the filter, submerge it in a bucket of water. If you run it out of water, it will burn out. (The same applies to submersible heaters, see page 36.)

AN INTERNAL POWER FILTER

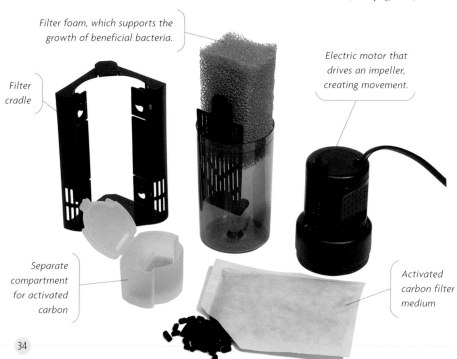

Filter foam, which supports the growth of beneficial bacteria.

Filter cradle

Electric motor that drives an impeller, creating movement.

Separate compartment for activated carbon

Activated carbon filter medium

INSTALLING AN INTERNAL POWER FILTER

Attach the carrier to the rear corner of the aquarium, pressing it firmly against the glass. Take care not to force the filter into the carrier or you may break the carrier.

Position the filter with the nozzle facing outwards. Direct the outflow across the diagonal of the aquarium.

Position the filter head at or just below the water surface (check the manufacturer's instructions).

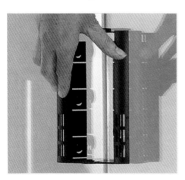

Allow a gap between the base of the filter and the substrate to avoid the accumulation of dirt and debris and to allow free passage of water into and around the filter canister.

EXTERNAL POWER FILTERS

Generally larger than internal filters, external filters are housed outside the tank and have the capacity to house different types of media for mechanical, biological and chemical filtration. These are often housed in separate compartments inside the filter body. For optimum flow, position an external filter as close to the water level as possible – typically in the cabinet underneath the aquarium – and minimize the hose lengths.

Arrange the filter media in the canister with the coarse filter foam at the bottom followed by a layer of biological medium, the carbon and, finally, a wad of filter wool.

Heating and Lighting

To replicate the natural environment of your fish as closely as possible, keep them in good health and allow you to enjoy them at their best, you will need to provide both heating and lighting in the aquarium. Both are easy to install but you will need to monitor the heater closely.

Heating the aquarium

A submersible combined heater-thermostat is the best bet for new fishkeepers: it is simple to regulate and is not easily tampered with once the correct temperature has been set. Some models have a light to indicate whether it is on or off: make sure you can see this.

The size of heater you will need (wattage) depends on the size of your aquarium. As a rough guide, you should allow 50 watts per 27 litres (6 gallons) of water in the aquarium. (See page 29 for tank capacities.)

Also available are separate submersible heaters and heating cables or mats, which need to be placed in the tank first, under the substrate. All these types need to be controlled by a separate thermostat, either external or submersible.

Monitoring the temperature

Check the temperature twice a day using an external or internal thermometer attached onto the tank. Expect temperatures to fluctuate by a degree or so but keep a record so that you can see if a problem develops.

INSTALLING THE HEATER

Place the heater at an angle with the heating element at the bottom so that as the heat rises it does not go straight past the thermostat.

The suckers are usually supplied detached from the unit. Slide them over the heater so that one is at the top and the other at the bottom. You may need to wet them to stick them to the glass.

Leave a gap between the bottom of the heater and the substrate. Do not cover units with substrate or they will overheat. Make sure the water flow is not obstructed by any tank decorations placed in front of the heater.

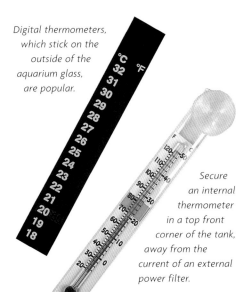

Digital thermometers, which stick on the outside of the aquarium glass, are popular.

Secure an internal thermometer in a top front corner of the tank, away from the current of an external power filter.

Lighting the aquarium

In the aquarium, lights perform the dual function of providing light energy for your plants to flourish and illuminating the display so that your fish can feel at home and you can enjoy the result.

Most modern aquariums come with fluorescent lighting tubes already integrated into the hood and this is certainly the easiest system to choose if you are new to fishkeeping. Always use lighting equipment specifically designed for use with aquariums, both from a safety and an efficiency standpoint.

Aquascaping – adding rocks and wood

Creating an effective display in your aquarium is not difficult: the main thing to remember is to keep it simple. Use only a few large pieces of wood and rocks – too many different types will look unnatural and will overcrowd the tank.

Preparing wood

The safest option is to buy pieces of bogwood, cork bark or Mopani wood directly from your aquarium shop, which should have a wide selection of sizes, shapes and colours.

First brush the wood thoroughly to remove any dust and dirt, then submerge it in a bucket of water. Change the water when it looks like strong tea and continue to do this until the water remains clear. This process may take up to two weeks.

Place the wood in the aquarium. You may need to weigh down pieces of cork and smaller pieces of bogwood to prevent them from floating.

SUITABLE ROCKS FOR THE AQUARIUM

Aquarium shops stock many types of rocks and stones but not all are suitable for a tropical freshwater aquarium. Those shown below are inert and will not affect the water chemistry. Scrub them well before placing them in the aquarium.

Rounded boulders
Can have great impact and make good grazing spots for algae-eaters.

Granite
The unusual sparkling texture will appear more natural with time.

Slate
Available in a variety of sizes.

Westmorland rock
An attractive reddish colour and striking markings.

Slate chippings
Chippings of other rocks may be available too.

Lava rock
Broken pieces create an unusual substrate.

Washed coal
Good for creating a dark display.

Small round pebbles
Ideal for creating a riverbed.

A BASIC AQUASCAPE PLAN

Before placing any décor in the aquarium, it is a good idea to sketch out an overhead plan showing where you want to put the various pieces.

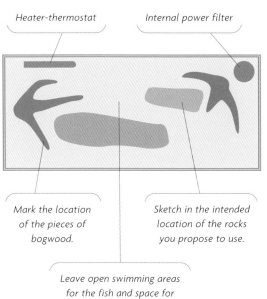

Heater-thermostat

Internal power filter

Mark the location of the pieces of bogwood.

Sketch in the intended location of the rocks you propose to use.

Leave open swimming areas for the fish and space for plants to flourish.

CREATING A REALISTIC DISPLAY

- Place rocks so that the strata run horizontally in the same direction.
- Securely anchor wood, especially buoyant pieces.
- Position root-shaped wood vertically to give the impression that it is part of a tree above the aquarium.
- Use smaller pieces of rock or wood to divide or define plant-growing areas.
- Use background décor to hide aquarium equipment.
- Remember that empty space is not necessarily a bad thing; it allows growing room for plants and a swimming area for fish.

This effective display uses only a few large pieces to create great impact. The natural 'cave' formed by the wood will be a welcome retreat for fish.

Water – treating, adding and testing

Once you are happy with the display of rocks and wood you have created in the aquarium, it is time to add the water. Tap water is generally safe to use provided that you first treat it with a proprietary water conditioner to remove chemicals that may be harmful to your plants and fish. Bacteria starter products are also available to help trigger biological cycles in the aquarium.

A proprietary water conditioner will neutralize chemicals harmful to fish contained in ordinary tap water and make it safe for aquarium use.

Keep a bucket solely for aquarium use so you can be sure it contains no residues of cleaning products.

Filling the aquarium

Use a clean jug to start filling the aquarium. Gently pour the water over a flat stone to avoid disturbing the substrate. If your display does not include one, carefully place a saucer into the aquarium and pour the water onto that. As the water level rises, you can gently pour the water from a clean bucket but be careful not to disturb the substrate. (However careful you are, the water is bound to look cloudy at first.) Fill the aquarium to only two thirds of its full capacity to allow plenty of room for water movement and displacement when you position the plants.

tip *Avoid moving a full aquarium*
Once an aquarium is full of water, it should not be moved. If you ever need to move it, you will need to empty it first of water, substrate, ornaments and fish.

MEASURING TANK VOLUME

Although it is not difficult to measure the volume of a rectangular tank (see page 29), this does not take into account the displacement caused by the substrate, aquarium equipment and décor in your particular aquarium display. You can measure the volume of your tank accurately by using a bucket of a known capacity. When the tank is roughly two thirds full, record the water volume so far. Knowing exactly how much water the tank holds is vital if you need to treat sick fish with medication diluted according to the volume of the aquarium.

*Pour the water slowly and carefully from a clean
jug onto a large flat stone in the aquarium to
avoid disturbing the substrate.*

USING TEST KITS

As we have seen (pages 8–9), it is vital to control
the water conditions in the aquarium if your fish
and plants are to remain healthy. Today's water
testing kits are simple to use and provide
accurate results. Carry out water tests before
adding fish to the new aquarium to check that
the filter is working properly and that water
conditions are stable and continue to test
every 7–14 days.

To ensure accurate results,
rinse the vial from the test
kit in aquarium water rather
than tap water and follow the
instructions carefully.

*The test card below
provides readings for (from
left to right) ammonia,
nitrite, nitrate and pH.*

Aquarium Plants – creating a display

The choice of aquatic plants is enormous and adding them to your aquarium is one of the most creative aspects of setting up your display. Your first consideration should be the size of your aquarium and the type of display you want to create. As with choosing fish, make sure you check the mature height and spread of the plants: you don't want to include ones that will have outgrown your aquarium in six months time.

Planning your planting

If you have made a plan showing where major pieces of rock and wood should go (see page 39), you can add to this now to create a structure for your planting.

The background should be dominated by the tallest species, ideally growing up to the water surface. Midground plants form the heart of the display and probably encompass the widest choice of suitable species. They should grow to about half the height of the aquarium. Midground planting should allow swimming space for the fish in the centre yet provide sufficient cover for the most timid species.

The foreground should feature low-growing species that will help to frame what is behind and achieve a natural look to the planted aquarium. Most of these species are rampant growers once established and will need regular pruning to keep them under control.

A SAMPLE PLANTING SCHEME

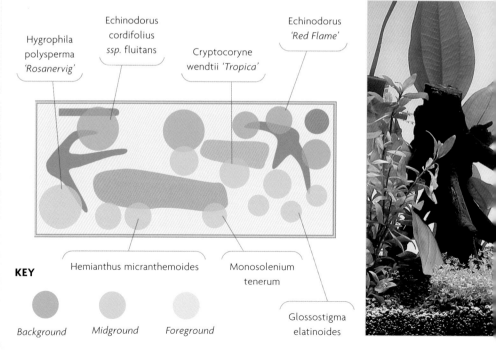

Hygrophila polysperma 'Rosanervig'

Echinodorus cordifolius ssp. fluitans

Cryptocoryne wendtii 'Tropica'

Echinodorus 'Red Flame'

Hemianthus micranthemoides

Monosolenium tenerum

Glossostigma elatinoides

KEY

Background

Midground

Foreground

Buying plants

Most aquatic stores will have a good selection of tropical aquarium plants for you to choose from. The plants should be displayed in easy-to-view clean tanks and labelled with details of their mature height and spread, price and, ideally, a guide to the best planting position in the aquarium: background, midground, etc.

Examine the plants carefully and reject poor specimens. A healthy plant will have hole-free leaves and roots and small plantlets growing through the base of the pot. Avoid any plants with brown or damaged leaves: yellow patches indicate a lack of nutrients.

Here, large Echinodorus *create a structural background, while* Cryptocoryne *define the midground area and will soften rock edges. Low-growing* Glossostigma *and* Hemianthus *leave swimming space for the fish.*

tip *Plant in groups*

If you have the space, you will create the best effects by using plants in groups of three or more of the same species.

When you have chosen your plants, the retailer should wrap them in individual bags that will then be filled with air to prevent the leaves being crushed during transit.

PREPARING A POTTED PLANT

This is a healthy Echinodorus 'Red Special' – note the strong roots that are growing out of the pot.

1 Cut the sides of the pot, in several places if necessary, and carefully peel away the pot to reveal the rockwood growing medium without damaging the plant.

2 Gently pull away as much of the growing medium from the roots as you can, taking care not to damage the roots.

3 If the roots are too long, trim them with sharp scissors so that you can spread them out when you come to plant them.

4 Remove any damaged leaves and make sure there are no snails or evidence of snail eggs, which will appear as blobs of jelly on the leaves.

Planting

When you have decided on the position of the plant in the aquarium, look at it from different angles to see if it has a natural 'front' face.

Placing plants in the aquarium takes some practice, but if possible learn to work one-handed. Holding the base of the plant in one hand, use one or two fingers to make the planting hole and then push the plant in and backfill with gravel.

tip

Leave room for growth

Don't be tempted to fill the aquarium with plants straight away. Allow existing plants to spread naturally; if gaps remain you can always add more plants later on.

Gently firm each plant into the substrate so that it does not tilt or fall over.

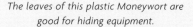

PLASTIC PLANTS

Plastic plants are much easier to care for than real ones and can look surprisingly realistic. However, although they are useful in an aquarium with fish that continually uproot real plants, they will do nothing to assist in the removal of nitrates from the tank. If you use plastic plants in your display you will need to pay particular attention to regular water changes and the efficiency of your filtration system.

The leaves of this plastic Moneywort are good for hiding equipment.

Simply click pieces together to change the length of the stems.

Sink the tray into the gravel to hold it in place.

Adding Fish – choosing the right ones

Having set up your aquarium display with equipment, décor and plants, it is tempting to go straight out and buy your fish. Resist the temptation! The filter will take about six weeks to mature biologically and the plants will need to establish themselves too. Wait at least a week before you introduce any fish, and then only buy a few – a maximum total fish length (excluding tail) of 25cm (10in) for an aquarium 60–90cm (24–36in) long or 38cm (15in) of total fish length for one 120cm (48in) long.

Choosing where to buy fish

The outlet where you buy your fish should sell good-quality, really healthy stock and it is worth visiting a few retailers to compare quality and price before you decide. A good shop and its tanks will be clean with no dead or diseased fish on show. The tanks should have labels detailing the fish species they contain, their price, potential size, any special food requirements, compatibility with other fish and any special requirements.

Choosing healthy fish

It is important to choose the healthiest fish and to judge this it is helpful to know what the species you are looking at normally looks like.

As well as checking the fish's appearance, look at how it behaves: its activity level, appetite, swimming position and tank level occupied should all be normal for the species and its respiratory rate should be relaxed not laboured. Certain types of behaviour, for example coughing, choking, yawning, scratching, shimmying or loss of swimming and/or buoyancy control, are normally indications of a problem.

A fish's eyes are usually a good indicator of its overall health – they should be alert and clear.

The fish's appearance, coloration and behaviour should be normal for the species. Avoid a fish that looks dull or sluggish.

tip

Leave your fish alone
It will take new fish a while to settle. Don't disturb or feed them for about 24 hours.

ADDING NEW FISH TO THE TANK

The retailer will place your new fish in a large plastic bag tied securely at the top. Always transport your fish directly home.

The corners of the bag should be taped to ensure that there is no risk of small fish becoming trapped.

1 When you arrive home, turn off the aquarium lights and float the bag unopened in the aquarium for 15 minutes.

2 Roll down the sides of the bag, add some aquarium water to the bag and leave it for a further 15 minutes.

3 Gently release the fish into the aquarium. Leave the aquarium lights off for a further hour.

Caring for Tropical Aquarium Fish

Enjoying your aquarium and keeping fish healthy

Provided that you have chosen your fish carefully and that you carry out regular water changes, tests and other maintenance tasks, caring for your fish should not be a difficult task. The two main causes of problems in the aquarium are incompatibility of fish – with other species or with their environment – and poor water quality. Carry out routine water tests and spend time regularly observing your fish and you will quickly see if a problem develops. The chart on page 57 provides advice on the possible causes of different symptoms and how to treat the problem.

Establishing a community

After your first fish and the filtration system have become established – they will need at least a few weeks – and provided that the results of water tests are acceptable, you can add a few more fish. Don't forget to check your total stocking level every time you buy new fish, and make sure that the new species you choose are compatible with the ones that you already have. Adding a new fish to an aquarium that has been set up for some time can lead to mayhem. Move around some of the rocks to dismantle established territorial boundaries.

REASONS FOR INCOMPATIBILITY

Before you decide on a particular species for your community aquarium, ask yourself the following questions about it.

● Is it, or will it be, too large for the aquarium or for other occupants?

● Is it territorial? Will it require more private space than the size of the aquarium can allow?

● Is it a piscivore (fish-eater) that may eat smaller fish in the aquarium?

● Is it so small that it may itself be eaten by larger fish already in the aquarium?

● Is it a fin-nipper? (This may not be a problem unless you also have species with long fins.)

● Is it too boisterous to fit in with sedate and/or nervous species, or vice versa?

● Is it likely to eat plants?

● Is it likely to dig up plants or otherwise rearrange the aquarium décor?

● Are its environmental requirements – water chemistry, movement and temperature – incompatible with those of existing species?

You will need to consider all these factors in conjunction.

tip *Carry out water tests*
Test for ammonia and nitrite levels regularly during the week following any fish introductions. This will allow you to take any remedial action necessary should the water quality deteriorate to an unacceptable level during this maturation process.

Corydoras catfish (see pages 18–19), Clown Loach (see page 15) and Cockatoo Cichlids (see page 61) are all popular subjects for a community aquarium.

Feeding – for good health

Aquarium fish require very little food but what they do need they will rely on you to supply. Overfeeding is more likely to be a problem than underfeeding – if uneaten food is left in the aquarium it will rot, leading to water quality problems.

Offer only a pinch of flake food at a time: it should be consumed within five minutes. For the first couple of months after setting up your aquarium, feed your fish only once a day to give the filter time to mature. Thereafter you can feed them twice daily.

The basic diet

The most practical food source for a community of tropical fish is a proprietary flake or pellet food. This will supply the fish's requirements for protein, fat or fatty acids, vitamins and carbohydrates and will also provide immune system stimulants.

Freeze-dried and frozen foods

Live foods, such as bloodworm, tubifex worms and daphnia, are sometimes offered for sale, but they may carry disease organisms that can infect your fish. Far better is to offer these foods in a freeze-dried or frozen form. Such foods are gamma-irradiated to kill fish pathogens before being either freeze-dried or frozen to maintain the nutrient content of the food.

Ideally, feed these foods to your fish as a treat in addition to their flake food diet. Allow frozen food to defrost before feeding it to the fish and do not refreeze it.

A VARIETY OF FOODS

Flake food is the most commonly available staple fish food.

These sinking pellets contain the same nutrients as flake food but are better for bottom-feeding species.

Offer only a pinch of flake food to start with. If your fish consume it in seconds, you can feed a bit more, but be careful not to overfeed.

tip Stick to the same diet

When you buy new fish, ask the retailer what type of food the fish have been accustomed to and continue the same regime at home. Make any changes to this diet gradually.

Standard flake food is also available pressed into a tablet form, designed to make it easier to watch the fish while they feed.

Tablet foods are similar to flake foods but pressed in a form that will adhere to the aquarium glass.

Freeze-dried tubifex is a safe way of offering this invertebrate food.

Freeze-dried mosquito larvae can form part of a more varied diet.

Algae wafers are ideal for herbivorous algae-eaters and bottom-feeding catfish.

Frozen foods are supplied in convenient blister packs.

A defrosted cube of bloodworm makes a good treat for fish.

Routine Aquarium Maintenance

In order to keep the aquarium – and, in particular, your fish – looking their best, it is important to establish daily, weekly and monthly maintenance routines. If you can, plan to carry out these basic tasks at the same time each day or week so that you don't overlook them. The chart on pages 54–55 provides a summary of these tasks.

It is also responsible practice to keep a record of when you complete tasks, as well as of the results of water tests, observations of your fish and any medication you administer to them. This will help you to spot any patterns and should enable you to deal with problems as soon as they arise.

Water changes

In order to dilute nitrates and other wastes that can build up in the aquarium, you will need to change approximately 15% of the aquarium water at least every other week. Well-stocked tanks or smaller aquariums will benefit from a weekly change of 20–25%. It is also important to remove dead algae and other residue to prevent it rotting down in the aquarium. Both tasks can be accomplished at the same time using a siphon-action gravel cleaner. The broad tube and wide foot allow you to 'hoover' a large area of the tank as you siphon out the water into a bucket. When you have finished, refill the tank with conditioned water (see page 40).

Move the siphon cleaner from one side of the aquarium to the other to remove organic debris in the substrate.

tip *Check for fish!*
Siphon cleaners should remove only lighter wastes while leaving the substrate relatively intact, but it is always a good idea to check that no small fish have been sucked up too.

CLEANING AN INTERNAL POWER

2 Over a bucket or bowl containing some aquarium water, open up the casing that houses the filter media, then remove the filter foam and put it in the bucket.

1 Switch off the electricity supply to the filter and unplug it. Carefully remove the internal power filter from its cradle.

3 Using filter wool dipped in aquarium water, wipe the casing inside and out, taking care to remove any plant fragments that have become trapped in the narrow slots.

4 Using fresh filter wool if necessary, clean all other parts, including the insert plate that holds the media in the filter, the impeller and its shaft and housing and the separate media compartment for activated carbon, if your filter has one. Check whether the impeller bearings need replacing.

5 Discard and replace the activated carbon, rinsing the new batch in a fine net held under running tap water.

6 Once you have cleaned all the parts, reassemble the filter in the order in which you dismantled it and replace it in the tank. Make sure that the unit floods fully – air trapped inside will stop the filter working properly.

ROUTINE MAINTENANCE TASKS

Daily

- Check the water temperature.
- Check for dead, damaged or distressed fish. Also look for early warning signs of ill health.
- Check that the internal filter is working properly.
- Feed the fish, making sure that they all receive their fair share.
- Check that the lights are working.
- Remove any uneaten food that fish do not seem interested in.

It only takes a minute to check that the filter is working properly.

Every 7–14 days

- Test the water for pH, ammonia, nitrite and nitrate levels.
- Clean the substrate with a siphon gravel-cleaner, making a 15% water change at the same time and refilling the aquarium with conditioned water at the same temperature.
- Clean the aquarium glass to remove the build-up of unsightly algae. An algae magnet will make this task easier.
- Remove dead or dying leaves from plants.
- Gently disturb fine-leaved plants to remove any trapped detritus.
- Feed plants with liquid fertilizer. (Make sure that you follow the manufacturer's instructions for correct dosing levels.)
- Where fitted, clean the condensation cover to avoid a reduction in light to plants.

Remove dead leaves from plants to prevent them decomposing in the water.

Plants as well as fish need feeding. Buy a proprietary fertilizer and follow instructions ▶

Every 4–6 weeks

- Clean the internal filter (see page 53), replacing expendable filter media.

Every 6–12 months

- Replace half the filter foam in the internal filter. Allow one month before replacing the other half.
- Replace fluorescent tubes, even if they are still working.
- Replace the filter pump impeller.

As necessary

- Replenish any tablet fertilizers for aquarium plants.
- Trim tall plants to prevent them blocking the light to lower-growing ones. (You can use the trimmings for propagation.)
- Check the quarantine tank (see pages 58–59) and make sure the filter is working properly in case the tank is needed for new fish arrivals or to treat existing stock.

A beautiful – and healthy – aquarium display like this is achievable provided that you perform routine maintenance tasks regularly.

Replace the filter foam when it no longer returns to its original shape when squeezed.

Make sure tall plants do not grow so much that they block the light from lower ones.

Health Care – symptoms and cures

Prevention is always better than cure, but even with proper aquarium maintenance, health problems may occur from time to time. If you have made a habit of watching your fish closely when they are well, you should be able to identify and treat problems quickly. Never ignore changes in a fish's appearance or behaviour.

tip

Keep water healthy

Most aquarium fish health problems are caused by poor water quality. If water conditions are poor, fish will be susceptible to all sorts of secondary infections.

SYMPTOMS TO LOOK FOR

Slime patches are caused by the fish's immune response to protozoan skin parasites. Other symptoms may include clamped, folded fins.

Very fine gold spots on the body are typical symptoms of velvet disease.

Skin damage can become infected with fungus to produce cottonwool-like growths on the body.

Cottonwool-like growths around the mouth could be symptomatic of a bacterial or fungal infection.

Swollen eyes may be the result of an internal bacterial infection or a tumour.

White spots on the skin are signs of a parasite infection called white spot.

Ragged edges to the fins may be caused by other fish or, particularly if fins are also red and sore, be signs of a bacterial infection known as fin rot.

Rapid gill movements may be an indication of water quality problems or be caused by parasites or a bacterial infection.

Swelling with scales protruding like a pinecone is commonly known as dropsy.

DIAGNOSING AND TREATING HEALTH PROBLEMS

Symptom	Causes	Treatment
Cottonwool-like growths around the mouth	A bacterial or fungal infection	Over-the-counter remedy that will treat both types of infection.
Swollen eyes	An internal bacterial infection	Over-the-counter bacterial remedy, or antibiotics (requires veterinary prescription in the UK).
Rapid gill movements	High ammonia and/or nitrite levels or other water quality problems. Parasitic or bacterial infection	Test water conditions. If these are good, try an over-the-counter external parasite or bacterial remedy or consult a veterinarian.
Ragged and/or bloody fins	Fin rot: a bacterial infection following physical injury or stress.	Over-the-counter fin rot remedy for mild cases. In more severe cases, consult a veterinarian.
White spots on the skin	A parasite infection called white spot – one of the most common fish health problems.	An over-the-counter white spot remedy will target the free-swimming stages of the parasite's life cycle and must be carried out over a period of a few days. Left untreated, it will spread to all the fish.
Protruding scales	A condition known as dropsy, caused by an internal bacterial infection that inhibits the fish's ability to control the level of water in its body.	An over-the-counter internal bacterial remedy
Cottonwool-like growths on the body	A fungal infection following skin damage.	An over-the-counter fungal remedy
Fine gold spots on the body	Velvet disease, caused by a skin parasite.	An over-the-counter targeted anti-parasite remedy.
Slime patches on the body	Caused by the fish's immune response to protozoan skin parasites.	An over-the-counter anti-parasite remedy
Flicking behaviour	See 'slime patches', above	See slime patches, above
Clamped, folded fins	See 'slime patches', above	See slime patches, above

Quarantining

A separate small tank is useful for quarantining not only sick fish but also new arrivals. This tank should measure at least 45x25x25cm (18x10x10in), but may need to be bigger than this for large fish. New fish should remain in the tank for 20 days, during which time you will need to monitor them closely.

If a fish becomes sick or distressed, it may benefit from being isolated in the quarantine tank, where you will be able to monitor its progress and treat it before returning it to the main aquarium. The tank can also be used as a breeding tank or nursery for the fry (see pages 62–63).

Using medications

Your aquatic dealer will stock many fish disease treatments and in most cases you will be able to treat the whole tank. Check that any treatment you buy is easy to use and has clear instructions on how to use any pipettes or measuring cups included, then follow these instructions precisely.

Carefully measure out the correct amount of treatment and add it to a clean jug filled with water taken from the aquarium. Mix the treatment into the water in the jug using a spoon that is free from any chemicals or other contaminants. Slowly pour the treatment over the surface of the aquarium. Diluting the mixture in this way will ensure an even distribution of the medication.

A QUARANTINE TANK

A simple internal sponge filter is ideal for a quarantine tank.

You will need an airpump to 'power' the internal sponge filter.

Always mix medication into aquarium water rather than tap water and check dosages carefully.

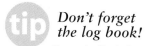 **tip**

Don't forget the log book!

Be methodical about recording in a notebook anything you do to the tank.

Use a heater-thermostat to maintain the water temperature at the same level as in the main display aquarium.

An internal or external thermometer will enable you to monitor the temperature.

Include a clean clay flowerpot or artificial décor item to provide a refuge for poorly or nervous fish.

Lay a thin substrate of gravel in the tank to help fish feel at home in their temporary quarters.

Keep a note of the volume of your aquarium

Knowing exactly how much water your tank holds (see page 40) is the only way you can administer medication accurately. Overdosing could be lethal to all your fish!

EUTHANASIA

If one of your fish is suffering from an untreatable condition, you may need to dispose of it humanely. The quickest and kindest way to do this is to sever its spinal cord just behind the head by cutting down with a very sharp knife. If you feel you can't do this yourself, consult a veterinarian. Do not flush it down the lavatory, which causes disease to spread to native fish populations. Neither should you put it in cold water or the freezer or adopt any other method that would cause your fish to suffer a long, lingering death.

Developing Your Hobby

Specialist aquariums, challenging species and breeding fish

When you have gained some experience in fishkeeping, you may want to think about keeping some more challenging species. If you have the space, you may even want to set up a second aquarium. In this book we have focussed on the community aquarium, but there are other fish you could consider for a single species tank. Or you could create a specific natural habitat, such as an Amazonian pool, African stream, Southeast Asian swamp or a brackish estuary, with fish and plant species that originate exclusively from that habitat.

Adding more 'difficult' fish

Once your community aquarium is established, you may decide to add some species that have more specific needs – they may require security provided by established plants, for example. Species that are inclined to be territorial will be less likely to regard the tank as their exclusive territory if they are added once other fish are established.

As when you first set up the aquarium, make sure that you have enough space and that these fish are compatible with the tank's existing occupants (see page 49).

tip *Always check compatibility*
Avoid keeping predatory fish with small fish that they are likely to eat, or keep them in a species tank that caters for their needs. Do your homework and take the professional advice of your local retailer regarding compatibility.

Cockatoo Cichlid

Apistogramma cacatuoides
Mature size: males up to
9cm (3¹⁄₂in), females up to
5cm (2in).
Both the male (shown right)
and smaller female (shown
above) Cockatoo Cichlid
from the Amazon have
stunning coloration.
Avoid keeping them
with other cichlids unless
they are in a large aquarium.

Zebra or Imperial Plec

Hypancistrus zebra
Mature size: 15cm (6in)
This is a fairly recent
introduction to the
aquarium world, but it has
made a name for itself
quickly with its
dramatic markings.

TEN POPULAR FISH
FOR A MATURE TANK

● Red Phantom Tetra
(*Megalamphodus sweglesi*)
● Kribensis
(*Pelvicachromis pulcher*)
● Ram, or Butterfly Cichlid
(*Microgeophagus ramirezi*)
● Angelfish
(*Pterophyllum scalare*)
● Zebra or Imperial Plec
(*Hypancistrus zebra*)
● Glass Catfish
(*Krptopterus bicirrhis*)
● Three-lined Pencilfish
(*Nannostomus trifasciatus*)
● Marble Hatchetfish
(*Carnegiella strigata strigata*)
● Lyretail Killifish
(*Aphyosemion australe*)
● Boeseman's Rainbowfish
(*Melanotaenia boesemani*)

Angelfish

*Pterophyllum
scalare*
Mature size:
15cm (6in)
This has been a
firm favourite with
fishkeepers for generations
and many colour morphs have
now been bred. Unfortunately,
Angelfish have a habit of picking
off their smaller tankmates such as
Neon and Cardinal Tetras. Keep only
with peaceful community fish that are
more than 4cm (1¹⁄₂in) long.

Breeding Fish – and caring for fry

Even if you don't set out to breed fish, there is every chance that, given the right conditions, some of your fish will breed. Tropical aquarium fish fall into two categories: livebearers and egglayers. The first young fish you are likely to find in a community aquarium are the young of livebearers (see pages 22–3).

Livebearers

As their name implies, these fish give birth to live young. Because these young fish are larger than the fry that hatch from eggs, they have a better chance of survival in the community aquarium, though some will inevitably fall prey to other fish.

They will be able to pick at flake food, but to give them a better start you can feed them special liquid fry food.

Egglayers

Although these fish may well spawn in a community aquarium, it is unlikely, in most cases, that their tiny offspring will survive there. If you want to breed these fish, it is better to set up a small tank with whatever the particular species requires, for example fine-leaved plants, slate or a cave. A small tank as used for a quarantine or hospital tank (see pages 58–59) will suffice for most species.

You will need to condition the parent fish by feeding them the correct foods to bring them into spawning condition. Check the requirements of the fish you want to breed.

Some species make good parents; others will eat their young. Again, you will need to find out about the particular species you want to breed: you may need to move one or both parents back into the community aquarium after spawning.

Liquid fry foods for livebearers and egglayers contain the food in suspension.

Breeding Siamese Fighting Fish will need a well-planted tank to themselves. The male of the species blows bubbles among floating plants and plant debris to form a bubble nest.

This Butterfly Cichlid, or Ram, (Microgeophagus ramirezi) is protecting its fry in a 'nursery' area among the aquarium rocks.

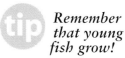

tip ***Remember that young fish grow!***

If fish breed and the fry survive, you will need to move them to another tank unless your stocking levels can cope with these extra bodies as they grow.

Zebra Danios are among the easiest egglaying species to breed. Adding cold water to the tank triggers a frantic spiralling courtship dance, after which fertilized eggs sink to the bottom. A layer of marbles will save them from parental predation.

A TANK FOR REARING YOUNG

A small tank, as used for a quarantine or hospital tank (see pages 58–59), can also function as a home for rearing fry. Partially fill it with water from the main aquarium and add a small amount of conditioned fresh water. In this way you can safely net and transfer the youngsters to the rearing tank without having to wait for the water to age. Keep feeding low until the filter has had a chance to build up enough bacteria to cope. Ideally, pre-mature a small air-powered sponge filter by running it in the main tank for at least a week.

Further Information

RECOMMENDED BOOKS

500 Ways to Be a Better Freshwater Fishkeeper
Bailey, Mary *et al* (Interpet Publishing, 2005)
Pet Owner's Guide to Tropical Fishkeeping
Bailey, Mary (Ringpress Books, 1998)
Tropical Fishlopaedia: A Complete Guide to Fish
Care Bailey, Mary and Burgess, Peter (Ringpress
Books, 2002)
Focus on Aquarium Fish: A Revealing Look at a
Vibrant Underwater World Rogers, Geoff and
Fletcher, Nick (Interpet Publishing, 2004)
An Essential Guide to Choosing Your Tropical
Freshwater Fish Sandford, Gina (Interpet Publishing)
A Practical Guide to Setting up Your Tropical
Freshwater Aquarium Sandford, Gina (Interpet
Publishing)
Setting Up a Tropical Aquarium Week-by-Week
Thraves, Stuart (Interpet Publishing, 2004)

MAGAZINES

Aquarium Fish (USA)
Freshwater and Marine Aquarium (FAMA) (USA)
Practical Fishkeeping (UK)
Today's Fishkeeper (UK) (formerly *Aquarist and
Pondkeeper*)
Tropical Fish (UK)
Tropical Fish Hobbyist (USA)
Tropical World (UK)

RECOMMENDED WEBSITES

http://badmanstropicalfish.com
http://www.skepticalaquarist.com
http://www.thetropicaltank.co.uk
http://www.tropicalfishfinder.co.uk
http://www.tropicalfishkeeping.com

PICTURE CREDITS

The majority of the pictures
in this book were taken by
Geoffrey Rogers and are the
copyright of Interpet
Publishing. Those on the
following pages were supplied
by and are the copyright of
www.photomax.co.uk: page
62(B), 63(T).